Internet Made Easy

Back Forward Home Reload Search Mail Print Folder

Internet
Scavenger Hunts
for the Topics You Teach

by Karen Leiviska

SCHOLASTIC
PROFESSIONAL **B**OOKS

New York ◆ Toronto ◆ London ◆ Auckland ◆ Sydney ◆ Mexico City ◆ New Delhi ◆ Hong Kong

Cover design by Norma Ortiz

Interior design by Ellen Matlach Hassell
for Boultinghouse & Boultinghouse, Inc.

Cover screenshots courtesy of Rainforest Action Network
(www.ran.org) and International Wolf Center (www.wolf.org)

Cover photo (wolf pups) by J. Westlund.

ISBN 0-439-17034-6

Copyright © 2000 by Karen Leiviska.

Printed in the U.S.A.

Contents

Introduction

Computer-related technology is increasingly becoming an integral part of our everyday lives. As educators we are expected to provide our students with the skills needed to advance in the world of technology. Teaching students to use the computer as a learning tool will equip them with the necessary skills to become productive members of the technological society of today and tomorrow.

The purpose of this book is to help teachers easily link technology to current curriculum goals and standards. In addition, completing the scavenger hunts will enhance students' reading and language arts skills. The topics included in this book are based on the content areas covered in the curriculum for grades 4–8. At least one hunt has been included for each topic. Select those that fit into your curriculum and use them in any order.

Though the information contained in each site is valuable and educational, please preview each site to make sure the material is suitable for the developmental level of your students. Bookmarking sites is a great way to lead them directly to the pages you want them to view.

The student activity pages can be used in a variety of ways. Students can work independently or in pairs, depending on your classroom access to the Internet. The only prerequisite Internet skills needed to successfully complete the activities include opening a browser, typing in a URL, and using the back and forward buttons. However, we provide detailed instructions, making it easy for students to implement the scavenger hunts independently, and giving them opportunities to practice their direction-following skills and increase their comfort in using the Internet.

Encourage students to answer questions using complete sentences when space allows. Writing in complete sentences will give them the opportunity to practice their paraphrasing skills. In many cases, the Web sites include plenty of information for your students to use to create more elaborate answers. For the most part, use the answer key as a guideline when reviewing your students' work. You will also find that these self-guided activities encourage creative, higher-level thinking.

Special note: One of the benefits of incorporating the Internet into your lessons is that your students can easily read up-to-the-minute information. However, this means that the layout and content of Web sites can also change. At the time this book went to press, the Web site addresses and content correlated to the information on the following student activity pages.

ANCIENT GREECE

To complete the chart below, choose to compare and contrast ancient Greek men and modern men or ancient Greek women and modern women. Make sure to use the information you read on the Web site, as well as what you have observed about men or women of today.

Men/Women OF ANCIENT GREECE	Men/Women OF MODERN _____ your state

Would you rather live in ancient Greece or in the present day? Why? _____

_____

_____

_____

_____

_____

Close your browser, or go on to the next section about Greek gods and goddesses.

ANCIENT GREECE

Greek Gods and Goddesses

Visit The A–Z of Greek Mythology Web site and learn about Greek gods and goddesses by typing in the following URL:

http://www.geocities.com/Athens/Olympus/7650/a-z.html

After arriving at this page, you will see the alphabet. Click on the first letter of the name of a god or goddess to find his or her section. Read about Zeus, Apollo, Athena, Demeter, and Hades. Then, answer the following questions.

1. Why is Zeus called "the father of Gods and the mortals"? _____

_____

2. Describe the birth of Zeus, according to an ancient myth. _____

_____

_____

3. What is one of the ways people viewed the characteristics of Zeus? _____

_____

_____

4. What gift did Apollo give to some mortals? _____

_____

5. Based on what you read, how would you describe Apollo's personality? _____

_____

_____

6. Athena was the daughter of _____.

7. How was her birth unusual? _____

_____

_____

Internet Scavenger Hunts   Scholastic Professional Books

ANCIENT GREECE

8. According to ancient myth, Athena gave several gifts to humans. Which one of these gifts do you consider the most important? Explain your answer.

_____
_____
_____

9. Demeter was the goddess of _____.

10. Why were the seasons affected by Demeter? Explain your answer. _____

_____
_____

11. Hades, brother of Zeus and Poseidon, is the god of the _____.

12. If you visited the world of Hades, describe what you might see and feel. _____

_____
_____

Read about any other gods or goddesses that interest you from this site. Next, choose one of them and describe how he or she would solve a problem that faces us in today's society.

_____
_____
_____
_____
_____

Close your browser, or go on to the next section about the ancient Olympics.

ANCIENT GREECE

Ancient Olympics

 Learn about the ancient Olympics by typing in the following URL:

http://www.perseus.tufts.edu/Olympics/

 After arriving at this page, click on the link **A Tour of Ancient Olympia**. Next, take the tour with pictures or QuickTime. While the QuickTime tour does include additional pictures, if you choose to take this tour, be patient: the movies take a lot of time to load. After you finish reading a section, click on the link **Next stop on the Tour**.

1. Describe Olympia, the setting for the Olympic Games for over a thousand years.

_____

_____

2. What was given to the winners of the ancient Olympics? _____

3. What was the first Olympic event? _____

4. How many events were included by classical times? _____

 Navigate back to the home page of this site by clicking on **Home**. Next, click on the link **Ancient and Modern Olympic Sports**. When you arrive at this page, read the information. Then, click on the links about the following sports and explain some of the characteristics or ways the sport in ancient times differs from the same one in present day.

5. Boxing _____

_____

6. Discus _____

_____

7. Jumping _____

_____

8. Running _____

_____

Internet Scavenger Hunts Scholastic Professional Books

ANCIENT GREECE ⬭⬭⬭

 Once again, navigate back to the home page of this site by clicking on **Home**. Next, click on the link **Athletes' Stories**. Read about the five athletes listed by clicking on each of the links. While you read, you can take notes about the athletes on a separate sheet of paper. Then, choose one athlete and a product used today that he might be hired to endorse and explain why.

_____

_____

_____

_____

⬭⬭⬭ After navigating through this site, complete the Venn diagram below comparing the ancient Olympics with today's Olympics.

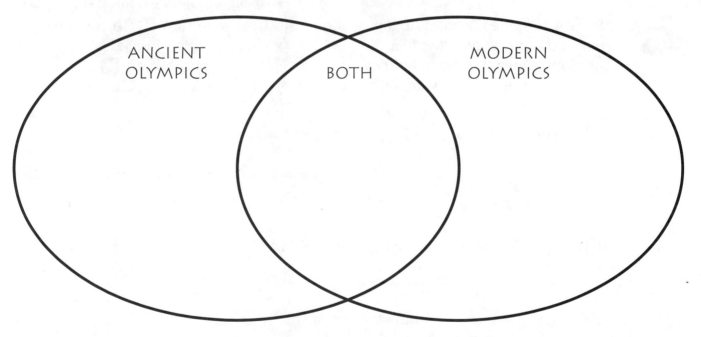

ANCIENT OLYMPICS   BOTH   MODERN OLYMPICS

9. Do you think it was harder to compete in the ancient Olympics, or is it more difficult today? If you could compete in an Olympic sport, which one would you choose?

_____

_____

_____

⬭⬭⬭ **Close your browser.**

The Human Body

Body Systems

 To learn about the human body systems, visit the <u>Brain Pop</u> Web site by typing in the following URL:

     http://www.brainpop.com

 Click on the link **Health Movies** on this page. Then, click on the link **Your Body**.

....

Hint: Preview the questions before watching the movie.

....

 When arriving at the next page, take the pop quiz while the movie is loading.

 After it has loaded, watch the movie about your body, and answer the following questions. Once the movie finishes, you will have the opportunity to watch it again.

TIP To pause the movie while you are watching, press the pause button ❚❚ .To continue watching the movie, press the play button ▶ .

1. The human body has _____ body systems.

2. The _____ system sends messages to the brain through

   a network of nerves.

3. Body growth and reproduction are controlled by hormonal glands which are contained

   in the _____ system.

4. Describe the function of the digestive system. _____

   _____

   _____

5. The _____ system removes chemical waste from cells.

6. Through breathing, the respiratory system exchanges _____

   for _____.

Internet Scavenger Hunts   Scholastic Professional Books

The Human Body

7. Oxygen and nutrients get to the parts of the body that need them through blood pumped by the _____ system.

8. Describe the function of the immune system. _____

_____

_____

9. Body tissue collects germ-fighting cells because of the _____ system.

10. The bones that hold up your body and protect the vital organs are called the

_____ system.

11. The _____ system allows your body's movement.

12. The_____ system consists of hair, skin, and nails.

13. How do body systems depend on each other? _____

_____

_____

_____

_____

_____

_____

Fun Fact!

What did Ancient Egyptians use instead of rulers to measure things? _____

_____

Close your browser, or continue with the next scavenger hunt that concentrates on keeping your body healthy.

Name _____ Date _____

The Human Body

Fitness

 To learn about fitness, visit <u>The Fitness Files</u> Web site by typing in the following URL:

http://mainetoday.webpoint.com/fitness/

 Once you arrive at <u>The Fitness Files</u>, click on the link **Fitness Fundamentals**. Then, click on **Benefits of an Active Lifestyle**.

The first benefit of keeping active is increased athleticism. Read about this benefit and the seven others found on this page. On the lines below, list each of the other benefits.

1. <u>increased athleticism</u>   5. _____

2. _____   6. _____

3. _____   7. _____

4. _____   8. _____

9. Circle the benefit you think is the most important and helpful. Explain your

choice. _____

_____

_____

_____

_____

_____

 To continue, click on the link **Fitness Fundamentals**. Then, click on the link **Do's and Don'ts**.

Internet Scavenger Hunts Scholastic Professional Books

The Human Body

Fitness Do's and Don'ts

On this page, there are some Do's and Don'ts that people should remember when beginning an exercise program. List them in the correct column.

DO ...	DON'T ...

When you have finished, click on the link **Fitness Fundamentals**. Then, click on the link **Fitness Myths.**

TIP Be sure to list all the fun ways that you like to exercise in the **DO** column!

Name _____ Date _____

The Human Body 🏃

The Myths of Fitness

🏃 This page contains twelve myths about a physical fitness routine. Click on each link. Then, fill in either True or False for the following statements.

1. _____ The best way to get fit is to run.

2. _____ Exercising only a short while each day has enormous benefits.

3. _____ As long as you're careful, warming up before you work out isn't necessary.

4. _____ A lifelong pattern of exercise is a great way to lose weight.

5. _____ If you don't feel any pain while you are exercising, it probably isn't doing you any good.

6. _____ The best way to help injuries feel better and heal faster is with heat.

7. _____ If you tape an injury, you should continue to play.

8. _____ The foods you ate yesterday provide energy for your workout today.

9. _____ The best time to exercise is always early in the morning.

10. _____ Your body needs water before, during, and after you work out.

11. _____ You can build strength fast by exercising the same body part every day.

12. _____ Women will develop big, bulky muscles if they lift weights.

Click on the link **Fitness Fundamentals**. Then, click on the link **Your Target Heart Rate** and read the page.

Heart Rates and Getting Active

You can figure out your target heart rate by typing in your age and clicking on the **Submit** button.

1. What is your maximum heart rate? _____

2. What is your minimum heart rate? _____

Internet Scavenger Hunts Scholastic Professional Books

The Human Body

3. While working out, your current heart rate should remain _____

_____ .

4. Explain how you can figure out your own heart rate. _____

_____

_____

_____

_____

_____

5. Try it! What is your current heart rate? _____

 Click on the link **Fitness Fundamentals**. Then, click on the link **Take the Fitness Quiz**. Read each question, click on the button next to the answer that you think is correct, and click **Submit**. You'll receive immediate feedback as to whether you answered each question correctly. After each question, click the link **On to the next question**.

 After you have answered all eight questions, click on the link **Get Active!** Then, click on the link **Finding the Right Activity**. Read the guidelines and keep them in mind while you are on your way to a fit lifestyle.

6. What is the main secret to sticking to your fitness program? _____

_____

_____

_____

7. The acronym DIF stands for _____

_____ .

 To go to the next section, click on the link **Fuel for Fitness**.

The Human Body

My Own Food Pyramid

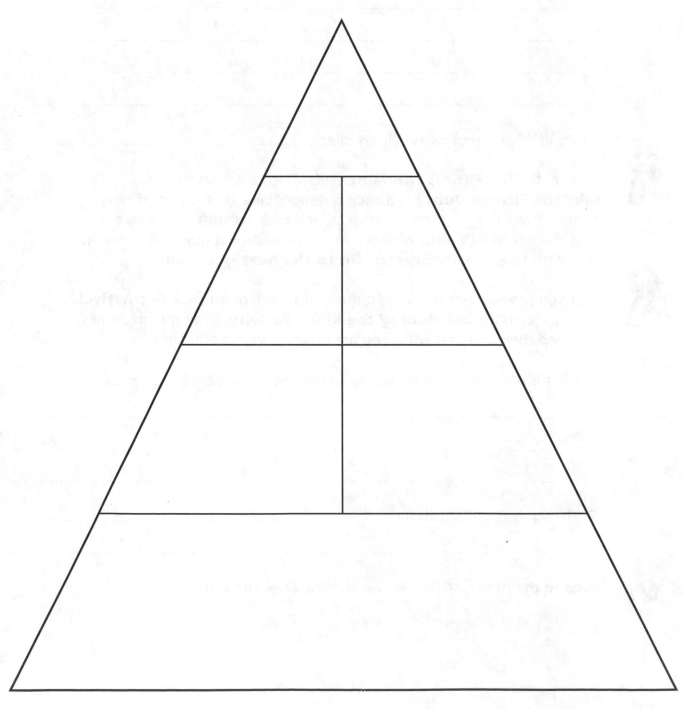

Click on the link **The Food Pyramid**. Read the information and then illustrate and label your own food pyramid. Be sure to include examples of the things you like to eat! Remember to mention how many servings a person needs from each group every day. When you have finished, click on the link **Get Active!** to go on to the next section.

Internet Scavenger Hunts Scholastic Professional Books

Name _____ Date _____

The Human Body

Calorie-Burning Comparison Chart

The link **Compare Calorie-Burning Workouts** will take you to a page called <u>The Calorie Burner</u>. Read the first paragraph. Then, enter your weight to find out how many calories you would burn doing different exercises. Fill in the chart below. Be sure to include activity/time combinations of your choice and write down how many calories they will burn. Put a ★ next to the activities you would enjoy the most.

SPORT	TIME	CALORIES
Playing basketball	45 minutes	
Skating	30 minutes	

Close your browser.

Martin Luther King Jr.

The Life of Martin Luther King Jr.

Visit the <u>Martin Luther King Jr.</u> Web site by typing in the following URL:

http://www.seattletimes.com/mlk/

Once you arrive at this page, click on the link **The Man**. Then, click on the link **Thirty-nine years for freedom:**, which provides a time line for many important dates and events related to Martin Luther King Jr. Read each date and event. Then, describe what happened on these dates that made them so important.

1. January 15, 1929 _____

2. 1948 _____

3. June 18, 1953 _____

4. 1958 _____

5. 1962 _____

6. August 28, 1963 _____

7. December 10, 1964 _____

8. February 9, 1965 _____

9. April 4, 1968 _____

10. January 20, 1986 _____

When you have finished, click on the link **The Man**. Then, click on the link **The Movement**.

Internet Scavenger Hunts   Scholastic Professional Books

Name _____   Date _____

Martin Luther King Jr.

===

Charting the Course of the Civil Rights Movement

 When arriving at the next page, click on the link **Fighting for fairness:**, which provides a brief time line for the civil rights movement. Read each date and event. Then, complete the chart below by adding seven events to the one that has been included to help you get started. Next to the events you add, describe why you think they are important.

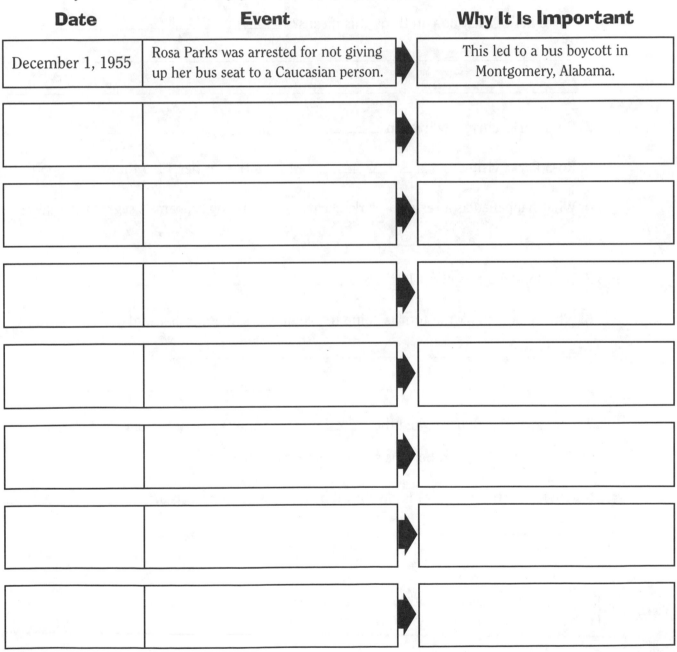

Date	Event		Why It Is Important
December 1, 1955	Rosa Parks was arrested for not giving up her bus seat to a Caucasian person.	▶	This led to a bus boycott in Montgomery, Alabama.
		▶	
		▶	
		▶	
		▶	
		▶	
		▶	
		▶	

When you have finished, click on the link **The Movement**. Then, click on the link **The Legacy**.

Martin Luther King Jr.

===

Rosa Parks

When arriving at the next page, click on the link **The fight's not over:**, an article about Rosa Parks that appeared in the *Seattle Times* newspaper on April 11, 1996. Then, answer the following questions.

1. At 83 years old, Rosa Parks has spent half her life being the "mother" of the civil rights movement. What do you think this means? _____

_____

_____

2. Rosa Parks currently lives in _____ .

3. Rosa Parks visited _____ cities on her 1996 tour.

4. What happened as a result of Parks's arrest for violating Alabama's segregation laws?

_____

5. How long did this event last? _____

6. Why do you think the tour is going to extend the same number of days? _____

_____

_____

7. December 1, 2000, marked the _____ anniversary of the day Rosa Parks refused to relinquish her bus seat to a Caucasian person.

8. What do you think Rosa Parks meant by her last quote in this article? _____

_____

_____

 If time permits, click on other links at this site to read more about Martin Luther King Jr. and the civil rights movement.

 Close your browser. Then, complete the questions on the next page.

Internet Scavenger Hunts Scholastic Professional Books

Name _____   Date _____

Martin Luther King Jr.

==

Think About It...

 Martin Luther King Jr. was only fifteen when he entered college. Predict what you will be doing when you are fifteen.

_____

_____

_____

 Dr. King believed in using nonviolent ways to change unfair laws and practices. What nonviolent ways can you think of to settle arguments with other people?

_____

_____

_____

 When someone threw a bomb into his house, Dr. King's followers wanted to fight. Instead, Dr. King said, "We must meet hate with love." What do you think that means?

_____

_____

_____

 Dr. King is referred to as a civil rights leader because he fought to win civil rights for African Americans. What does the term *civil rights* mean to you?

_____

_____

_____

 Dr. King dreamed of a world free of hate, prejudice, and violence. With a partner, brainstorm words and phrases that describe your ideal world.

_____

_____

_____

Name _____ Date _____

The Nine Planets

Facts About the Solar System

 Visit <u>The Nine Planets for Kids!</u> Web site by typing in the following URL:

http://www.planets4kids.com/

 When arriving at this page, click on the link **Let's Go!** and read to find the answers to the following questions.

1. There are _____ planets in our solar system. These planets travel in

circular paths called _____ around the sun.

2. The four planets in the inner solar system are _____

_____.

3. Why do you think the terms *inner solar system* and *outer solar system* are used when

referring to the placement of the planets in our solar system? _____

_____

4. What separates the inner and the outer planets? _____

_____

5. Use the space below to illustrate and label the sun, nine planets, and the asteroid belt.

Internet Scavenger Hunts Scholastic Professional Books

The Nine Planets

Planets and Their Characteristics

Click on the rocket and read the next page. Then, add the characteristics that describe the categories to the web below. Remember to list the names of the planets in the correct category.

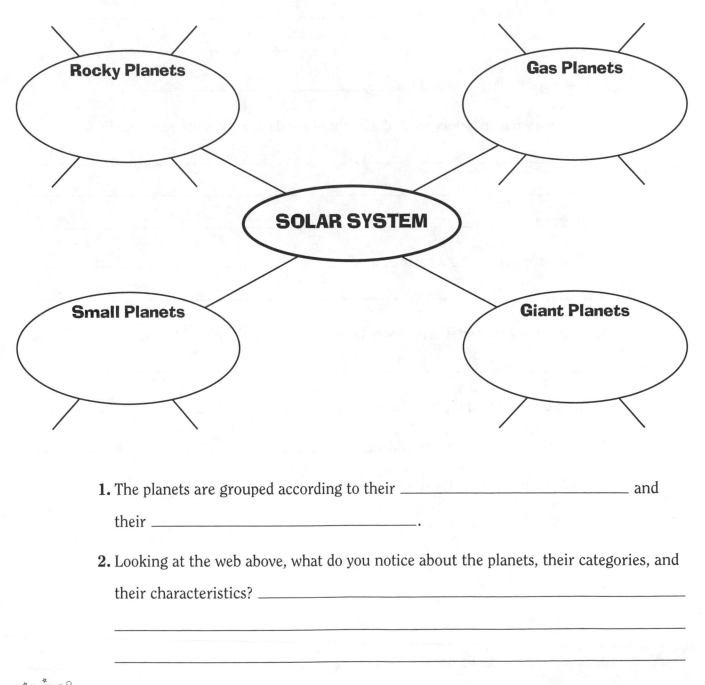

1. The planets are grouped according to their _____ and

   their _____ .

2. Looking at the web above, what do you notice about the planets, their categories, and

   their characteristics? _____

   _____

   _____

Explore the nine planets by clicking on the link at the bottom of the page.

The Nine Planets

The Sun and Inner Planets

To learn more about the sun and inner planets, click on each of the links, read the sections, and answer the following questions.

TIP When you have finished reading a section, click on **Explore More Planets!** to return to the list of links.

1. What is a heliocentric system? _____

_____

2. The sun's surface is called the _____.

3. Describe what sunspots are and why they look darker than the rest of the sun.

_____

_____

_____

4. What happens during a solar eclipse? _____

_____

5. What are the diameter and center temperature of the sun? _____

_____

6. The spacecraft that visited Mercury was named _____.

7. Recently, radar has shown evidence of _____ at Mercury's north pole.

8. How was the Caloris Basin probably created? _____

_____

9. From this page, list another fact about Mercury you think is interesting.

_____

_____

10. Describe how Venus probably got its name. _____

_____

_____

The Nine Planets

11. The greenhouse effect is the cause of Venus's hot temperature. Explain this theory.

_____

_____

_____

_____

12. Write two ways Venus is similar to and different from Earth.

Similarities	Differences

13. What is meant by "Earth's surface is very young"? _____

_____

14. Name at least two important facts about the water on Earth.

_____

_____

15. How has viewing Earth from space helped humans? _____

_____

_____

_____

16. People sometimes call Mars the _____.

17. Describe the spectacular feature, Olympus Mons. _____

_____

_____

18. Evidence suggests that _____ may once have existed on Mars.

The Nine Planets

The Outer Planets

To learn more about the outer planets, click on each of their links. Then, read the sections and answer the following questions.

1. Why does Jupiter appear to have different colors? _____

_____

2. What do scientists believe about Jupiter's Great Red Spot? _____

_____

_____

_____

3. How many moons does Jupiter have? _____

4. Name the four Galilean moons. _____

_____

5. How are Saturn's bands different from Jupiter's? _____

_____

_____

6. Describe Saturn's rings. How are they different from the rings of other gas planets?

_____

_____

_____

7. How many moons is Saturn known to have? _____

8. Do you think that any more will be discovered? Explain your answer. _____

_____

_____

_____

Internet Scavenger Hunts   Scholastic Professional Books

The Nine Planets

9. Why does Uranus appear to have a blue color? _____

_____

_____

10. How is Uranus different from most planets? _____

_____

_____

11. How is Neptune similar to and different from Uranus? _____

_____

_____

_____

12. What do scientists think about the disappearance of Neptune's Great Dark Spot?

_____

_____

_____

_____

13. Why do you think so little is known about Pluto? _____

_____

_____

_____

14. What would you like to know about Pluto? _____

_____

_____

_____

_____

The Nine Planets

Planet Comparisons

 Click on the link **Planet Pit Stop**. Next, click on the link
Compare the Planets! and answer the following questions.

1. Name the planet that has the longest year. _____

2. How many Earth days does that equal? _____

3. Name planet that has the largest diameter. _____

4. Approximately how many planets the size of Earth could fit into the largest planet?

_____

5. Name the planet or planets have neither rings nor moons. _____

_____

_____

 When you have finished, click the link to display the menu. Then, click
Back to Planet Pit Stop. When you arrive at the next page, click on
the link that will take you to the Weighing Station. Enter your weight and
click on the **Calculate** button to find out how much you would weigh on
each planet.

6. On which planet would you weigh the least? _____

7. On which planet would you weigh the most? _____

8. On which planet would you weigh the closest to what you weigh on Earth?

_____

9. What is the force that makes your weight change from planet to planet?

_____

_____

Close your browser.

Internet Scavenger Hunts   Scholastic Professional Books

Name _____   Date _____

The Rain Forest

What's in the Rain Forest?

 Visit the <u>Rainforest Action Network</u> Web site by typing in the following URL:

http://www.ran.org/

 When you arrive at the site, click on the link **Kids' Action Team**.
When you get to the next screen, click on **Enter**. Next, click on the
link **Rainforests are full of life!** to read about the people, plants,
and animals of the rain forest and how their lives are threatened.
Then, answer the following questions.

1. What have these tribal people taught us? _____

_____

_____

_____

2. Why are the plants of the rain forest so important to the medical world? _____

_____

_____

_____

_____

3. Why do the people who are accustomed to living in the rain forest often become very

ill when they are forced to move into cities? _____

_____

_____

_____

_____

The Rain Forest

Next, click on the **Kids' Corner** link. Then, click on **ANIMALS**. Read the Tropical Rainforest Animals page and answer the following questions.

4. What are some reasons why so many animals live in rain forests? _____

_____

5. On your first few steps into a rain forest, what animal would you probably see?

_____

_____

6. How can so many species of animals share the resources of the rain forest? _____

_____

_____

_____

7. Describe some positive ways plants and animals of the rain forest rely on each other.

_____

_____

_____

8. All species of animals in the rain forest have their own unique adaptations, or ways of helping them to survive. A walking stick and a boa constrictor have one adaptation in common. What is it? How does this benefit each animal?

_____

_____

9. What adaptation does the coral snake have for protection? _____

_____

10. Would you like to be a hoatzin in the rain forest? Why or why not? _____

_____

_____

Name _____ Date _____

The Rain Forest

Think About It...

 What can contribute to the extinction of animals in the rain forest? Explain your answer.

_____

_____

_____

 Some of the strangest, most beautiful, largest, smallest, quietest, and loudest animals live in the rain forest. Because so many fascinating animals live in the rain forest, millions have yet to be named or identified. Imagine that you are walking through a rain forest and have discovered a new species of animal. Name, describe, and illustrate this new animal.

_____

_____

_____

_____

_____

Name _____ Date _____

The Rain Forest

Rain Forest Layers and Locations

 To continue, click on the **Kids' Corner** link. Then, click on the link
Questions & Answers to complete the following.

1. Name and describe the three layers of life in a tropical rain forest. _____

_____

_____

_____

_____

2. Where are tropical rain forests located? Complete the following tasks on the map
below.

    ✔ Label the seven continents.   ✔ Draw and label the equator.

    ✔ Label the four major oceans.   ✔ Draw a compass rose on the map.

    ✔ Locate and color where rain forests still exist today.

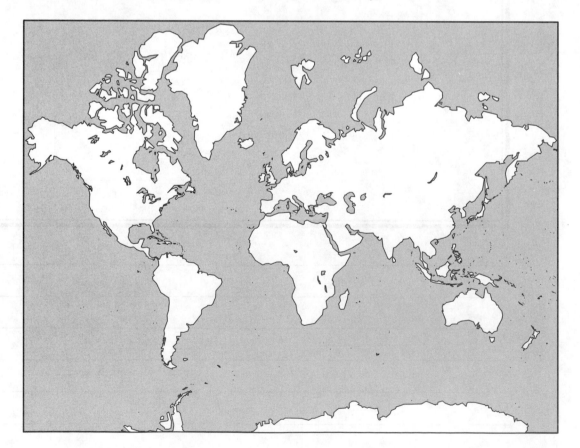

Internet Scavenger Hunts Scholastic Professional Books

The Rain Forest

Think About It...

In what way do rain forests help the entire world? _____

_____

_____

Why isn't a rain forest able to grow back? _____

_____

_____

To continue, click on the **Kids' Corner** link. Then, click on the link
7 Steps For Kids to Take and read the information. Think about what
you can do as an individual to help save the rain forests. Next, with a
small group, brainstorm and develop an action plan that will help save
the rain forests. Share your action plan with your class.

Rain Forest Action Plan

_____

_____

_____

_____

_____

_____

_____

_____

_____

_____

_____

_____

Name _____ Date _____

VOLCANOES

 Visit the <u>Volcano World</u> Web site by typing in the following URL:

http://volcano.und.nodak.edu

 When you arrive at the site, click on the link **VW Index**, which will take you to the VolcanoWorld Index. Click on the link **Lesson plans**.

 Once you have arrived at a page called Volcano Lesson Plans, first click on **Online lessons** and then click on **The Earth's Layers**, located under Chapter 1. To read through this lesson, click **Next**. Click the **Back** button if you need to review. Read the information on each page to answer the following questions.

Earth's Layers

1. Name the four layers of Earth. _____

_____

_____

_____

2. The layer of Earth we live on is called the _____.

3. The two types of rock that make up the crust are called _____.

4. The two heavy metals that make up the core are called _____.

··
Hint: Take some time to study any diagrams on these
pages. They can help you to understand what you read.
··

5. Earth's crust is about _____ miles thick under the oceans and about

_____ miles thick under the continents.

6. The deepest parts of the crust can reach up to _____ degrees F.

7. The crust of Earth is broken into many pieces called _____.

Internet Scavenger Hunts   Scholastic Professional Books

VOLCANOES

8. These plates usually float smoothly along the mantle, but at times they build up

pressure. What happens when this pressure snaps the rock? _____

_____

_____

9. Describe the difference between basalt and granite. _____

_____

_____

10. Describe the composition and temperature of the mantle. _____

_____

_____

_____

11. Geologists believe the mantle flows because of convection currents. Describe

convection currents. _____

_____

_____

_____

12. On the table below, describe the location, thickness, and temperature of the outer and
inner cores.

	OUTER CORE	**INNER CORE**
Location		
Thickness		
Temperature		

VOLCANOES

TIP **Other Lessons** will help you find your way back more quickly.

Volcano Facts

Navigate back to Earth Science Lessons. Then, click on **Volcanoes**, located under Chapter 2. When you arrive at the page containing the online lesson called Volcanoes, click on the **Next** button to learn more about volcanoes and answer the following questions.

1. What is the most powerful force in nature? _____
_____

2. Describe the origins of the word *volcano*. _____
_____
_____

3. Scientists use human terms when they talk about volcanoes. Name these terms.
_____
_____

4. What are the two definitions of the word *volcano*?

 • _____

 • _____

5. How tall did Paricutin grow in one week in 1943? _____

6. Volcanoes are classified as active, dormant, and extinct. Define these terms below.

Active	Dormant	Extinct

7. Look at the photographs of Mt. St. Helens before and after the eruption. What differences do you see? _____
_____
_____

Internet Scavenger Hunts Scholastic Professional Books

VOLCANOES

Volcanic Cones and Eruptions

 Navigate back to Earth Science Lessons. Then, click on **Volcanic Cones and Eruptions**, located under Chapter 3. When you arrive at the page containing the online lesson called Volcanic Cones and Eruptions, click on the **Next** button to begin. Read the passages and answer the questions below.

1. What are two reasons volcanoes erupt?

- _____
- _____

2. How are volcanoes classified? _____

_____

3. What are the three basic cone shapes? _____

_____

_____

4. What happens to the shape of the cone as the eruption becomes more violent?

_____

_____

_____

5. Describe an Icelandic, flood, or fissure eruption. _____

_____

_____

_____

6. Describe a shield cone. _____

_____

_____

_____

VOLCANOES

7. Illustrate a shield cone below.

8. What is a Strombolian eruption and what kind of cone does it create? _____
_____
_____
_____

9. Describe how a cinder cone forms. Then illustrate one below. _____
_____
_____
_____
_____

Internet Scavenger Hunts Scholastic Professional Books

VOLCANOES

10. Describe a Vulcanian eruption and name the type of cone it creates. _____

_____

_____

_____

_____

_____

_____

11. List six famous examples of this type of cone and where each is located.

- _____
- _____
- _____
- _____
- _____
- _____

12. Name and describe the most explosive type of volcanic eruption. Remember to include

an example. _____

_____

_____

_____

_____

_____

_____

_____

Close your browser.

Whales

Whale Facts

 Visit <u>Watery World of Whales</u> by typing the following URL:

    http://whales.magna.com.au/

After arriving at this page, click on the link **Whale FAQ**. Click on the appropriate links to find the answers to the following questions.

1. Why can't whales survive in fresh water?

_____

_____

_____

2. There are _____ different species of whales found in the oceans today.

3. Why might a whale swim faster than usual? _____

_____

_____

_____

4. The whale that can dive the deepest is called the _____.

5. How did the humpback whale get its name? _____

_____

_____

_____

6. Why are whales unable to breathe through their mouths? _____

_____

_____

_____

Whales

7. What is one reason why whales may have lost their sense of smell? _____

_____

_____

_____

8. What would happen to a whale if it went into a full deep sleep? Why? _____

_____

_____

_____

9. How long can whales stay underwater? _____

_____

_____

10. The maximum life span of the humpback whale is _____.

11. The maximum life span of the male killer whale is _____.

12. The maximum life span of the sperm whale is _____.

13. Why is the equator a natural barrier to larger whales? _____

_____

_____

_____

_____

Do you have a question that you would like answered about whales? First look through the list of FAQ (Frequently Asked Questions) to see if the topic is covered. If not, with your teacher's help, just click on the mailbox and send your question. The answer will be returned to your teacher's e-mail address.

_____

_____

Name _____ Date _____

Whales

Navigate back to the first page of <u>Watery World of Whales</u>, and click on the link **Photo Gallery**. Here you will find many photos of whales that can be enlarged by clicking on the images. Choose a whale to illustrate in the frame.

Close your browser, or go on to the next section about whales.

Internet Scavenger Hunts Scholastic Professional Books

Name _____ Date _____

Whales 🐋

All About Whales

🐋 Visit the <u>WhaleTimes SeaBed</u> Web site by typing in the following URL:

http://www.whaletimes.org

🐋 After arriving at this page, click on the link **Fishin' for Facts?**™ and then click on the links **Killer Whale**, **Blue Whale**, and **Gray Whale**. Read the passages to find out how big they are, what they eat, where they live, and other interesting facts. Complete the Venn diagram below using the information about two kinds of whales.

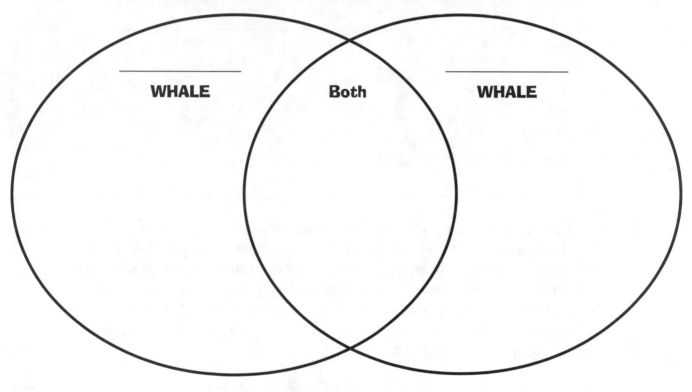

WHALE   Both   WHALE

Compare and Contrast

🐋 Using the information you organized above, write five sentences that compare and contrast the two whales you chose.

_____

_____

_____

_____

_____

Name _____ Date _____

Whales

Think About It...

 Think about how big a whale really is! Measure the length of your classroom and compare it to the lengths of the whales you have read about so far.

The length of my classroom is _____.

Click on the links on the Fishin' for Facts™ page and fill in the lines below.

- _____   _____
        whale name   length
- _____   _____
        whale name   length
- _____   _____
        whale name   length
- _____   _____
        whale name   length

Circle the whales that are longer than your classroom.

When you have finished, click on the link **KidsPage**. Then, click on the link **The Neverending Whale Tale**. This page contains a story that is being written by students from all over the world. Read the story, beginning with Chapter 1. You can continue reading the story by clicking on each of the chapter links. In small groups, think of 3–5 sentences to add to the story. Use the space below to write a rough draft. With your teacher's help, submit your paragraph to be added to the story.

_____

_____

_____

_____

_____

_____

_____

 **Close your browser.**

Internet Scavenger Hunts Scholastic Professional Books

Name _____   Date _____

The White House

Washington, D.C.

 Visit <u>The White House for Kids</u> Web site by typing in the following URL:

http://www.whitehouse.gov/WH/kids/html/home.html

 Click on the link **Where is the White House?** and read the page to answer the following questions.

1. The street address of the White House is _____.

2. Look at the map of historic sites on this page. What three places honor presidents?

_____

_____

3. What river is shown on the map? _____

4. Fill in the blanks below with *north, south, east,* or *west*.

- The Washington Monument is _____ of the White House.

- The Lincoln Memorial is _____ of the Washington Monument.

- The Capitol is _____ of the Washington Monument.

- The White House is _____ of the Jefferson Memorial.

 When you have finished, return to **White House for Kids**. Next, click on **The History of the White House**. Then, click on **Choosing a City**.

5. Who selected the location of our country's capital city? _____

6. Why was this location chosen? _____

_____

7. Describe what you might have seen if you were looking at the original

Washington, D.C. _____

_____

_____

Name _____   Date _____

The White House 🏛

White House Facts

🏛 Click on **White House History for Kids**.

1. The White House was the biggest house in the United States until _____
_____.

2. Name the president who served the shortest term. _____

3. How long did his term last? _____
_____

🏛 Click on **Constructing a Home for the President**.

4. The construction of the White House began in the year _____.

5. Name the first president to live in the White House. _____
_____

6. What happened to the White House while James Madison was president? _____
_____

7. What did James Madison's wife Dolley do to help? _____
_____
_____

🏛 Click on **The President's House**.

8. About how many visitors see the White House each day? _____

9. The White House has _____ floors, _____ rooms,
_____ bathrooms, and _____ doors.

10. Who gave the White House its current name? When did this occur? _____
_____
_____

Internet Scavenger Hunts   Scholastic Professional Books

The White House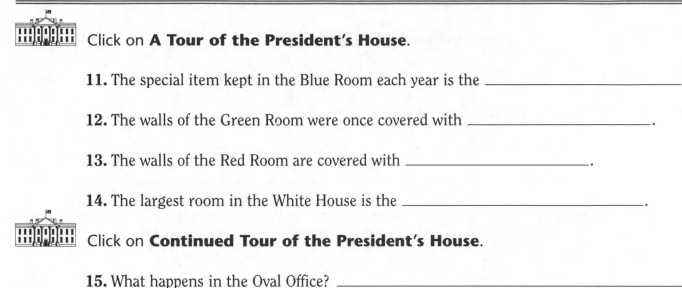

Click on **A Tour of the President's House**.

11. The special item kept in the Blue Room each year is the _____.

12. The walls of the Green Room were once covered with _____.

13. The walls of the Red Room are covered with _____.

14. The largest room in the White House is the _____.

Click on **Continued Tour of the President's House**.

15. What happens in the Oval Office? _____

_____

The People and Pets

Return to **White House for Kids**. Next, click on the link **Kids in the White House**. Read to answer the following questions.

1. President Kennedy's daughter Caroline had a pet named Macaroni that she often kept in the White House gardens. What kind of animal was it? _____

2. President Lincoln's youngest son Tad was known for his playfulness. What did he once do in the White House? _____

_____

 Click on **Pets in the White House**.

3. Who is Buddy and when did he arrive at the White House? _____

_____

4. Who is Socks and how long has he lived at the White House? _____

_____

5. What unusual pet did Russell Harrison have at the White House? _____

_____

The White House 🏛️

🏛️ Click on **More Pets in the White House**.

6. Of all the presidential pets you learned about on these pages, which one would you

like as a pet? Explain your answer. _____

_____

_____

_____

_____

_____

🏛️ When you have finished, click on **White House for Kids**.

7. Think of an area of concern in our country today, such as crime, violence, taxes, or the
environment, and use the space below to write a letter to the president expressing
your thoughts. Your teacher can help you e-mail your letter by clicking on the link
Write to the White House.

_____

_____

_____

_____

_____

_____

_____

_____

_____

_____

_____

🏛️ When you have finished, click on the link **White House for Kids** to continue.

Internet Scavenger Hunts Scholastic Professional Books

The White House

The Presidents

To learn about the presidents of the United States, click on the link
White House History. When you arrive at this page, click on the link
The Presidents of the United States. Select two presidents you would
like to read about and click on their links. Then, fill in the table below to
help you compare and contrast the presidents.

	_____ president	_____ president
Something you already know about this president		
Date of birth		
State of origin		
Party affiliation		
Number of terms served		
Dates of terms		
War fought during presidency		
Important accomplishment(s)		
Other fact(s) that interest you		
Something you would like to know about this president		

 Close your browser.

WOLVES

Wolf Facts

Visit the <u>International Wolf Center</u> Web site by typing in the following URL:

http://www.wolf.org

After arriving at the <u>International Wolf Center</u> home page, click on the link **Learn About Wolves**. At the next page, click on the link **FAQ's**. Then, click on the link **Basic Wolf Information**. Answer the following questions from information found on this page.

1. How many subspecies of the gray wolf are currently found in North America?

_____

2. Name at least three characteristics that differ between subspecies of the gray wolf.

_____

_____

_____

3. Describe a pack of wolves. _____

_____

_____

4. How many wolves are generally in a pack? _____

_____

5. Why does pack size vary so much? _____

_____

_____

_____

6. In which season are wolf pups born? _____

7. What is the average litter size of pups born each year? _____

WOLVES

8. Fill in the chart below.

LOCATION	WEIGHT	
	Adult Male	**Adult Female**
Northwestern Minnesota		
Northwestern United States, Canada, and Alaska		

9. Why do you think wolves weigh more in Canada, Alaska, and the northwestern United States than in other areas? _____

_____

10. Name at least two animals that are a primary food source for wolves. _____

_____

11. Name at least two animals that are a secondary food source for wolves. _____

_____

12. What animals, if any, are found in the area in which you live that are either a primary or secondary food source for wolves? _____

_____

13. How much food does a wolf require to reproduce successfully? _____

_____

14. What is the least amount of pounds of food a wolf must eat in a week in order to survive? _____

15. On average, wolves kill _____ deer in a year.

16. Describe the running pace of a wolf while chasing prey. _____

_____

_____

17. How far might a wolf travel in one day? Why? _____

_____

_____

18. Do wolves live longer in captivity or in the wild? Why do you think this happens?

_____

_____

_____

How Wolves Communicate

When you have finished, click on the link **Basic Biology**. Next, click on the link **Communication** and read this page to help you answer the following questions.

1. What do wolves use to demonstrate the rules of a pack? _____

_____

2. What is the most important rule in a pack of wolves? _____

_____

3. Describe the characteristics of alpha wolves and the role these wolves play in the

organization of a pack. _____

_____

_____

_____

4. How do alpha wolves communicate that they are leaders? _____

_____

_____

Internet Scavenger Hunts   Scholastic Professional Books

WOLVES

5. Use the space below to illustrate two wolves having a disagreement. Make sure your drawing shows the body language of the dominant wolf (the leader) as he rules over the subordinate wolf (the follower).

6. What is scent-marking? How are scents useful to wolves? _____

_____

_____

7. Name three reasons why a wolf might howl. _____

_____

_____

_____

8. Basically, wolves use three different languages. Name them. _____

_____

_____

9. What are ways you can think of that humans use body language? _____

_____

_____

_____

Name _____ Date _____

WOLVES

The crossword puzzle below is based on the information you have already read at the <u>International Wolf Center</u> Web site. If needed, review the information by rereading the sections.

Across

3. The _____ wolf lives in the highlands of Ethiopia in Africa.

4. Wolves use _____ language to convey the rules of the pack.

6. _____ are a primary food source for wolves.

8. Wolves mark their territories with urine and scats, a behavior called _____.

9. Very young wolves are called _____.

11. The leaders of the pack are known as _____ wolves.

13. There are _____ subspecies of the gray wolf in North America.

14. More than one offspring born to a female wolf at one time is called a _____.

15. If a wolf sticks its ears straight up and bares its teeth, it is _____.

Down

1. A less dominant wolf is called a _____.

2. _____ are a secondary food source for wolves.

4. Wolves _____ to warn other pack members of danger.

5. Wolves die primarily from _____.

6. Lower-ranking wolves hold their tails _____.

7. A wolf standing tall with its tail high communicates _____.

10. Wolves will occasionally _____ on birds.

12. In _____ and northwestern Canada, some wolf packs have over 30 members.

13. A wolf will show _____ by flattening its ears against its head.

Close your browser.

Internet Scavenger Hunts   Scholastic Professional Books

Answer Key

Ancient Egypt

The Pyramids and Ancient Egyptians
(pages 5–7)

1. pharaohs; gods

2. *Kemet* meant "black." This was the color of the silt-layered and fertile soil left behind each year when fields were flooded by the Nile.

3. Menes

4. Memphis was founded where Upper and Lower Egypt met—at the apex of the Nile.

5. Pyramids were built as monuments that contained the tombs of pharaohs.

6. Death was seen as the beginning of eternal life.

7. Answers may vary but should include the key idea that the things buried with a pharaoh were of a familiar nature.

8. A mastaba was a tomb that was covered, rectangular, made of mud and brick, and had a deep burial shaft. Mastabas held the bodies of those who were important in the court of a king.

9. The Step Pyramid was built for King Zoser.

10. He was the architect of the Step Pyramid.

11. The actual burial place was in a central area. Some of a king's possessions were placed in surrounding rooms. Though there were false doors, made of heavy stone and inscribed with hieroglyphs, there were no real doors or passageways between the rooms. It was believed that in the afterlife, a king would not need them to move from room to room.

12. the Great Pyramid

13. King Khufu commissioned the Great Pyramid, which took 30 years to build.

14. Papyrus twine was used to haul the stones up gradually sloping ramps.

15. Sphinx

16. Boats were meant to help transport the pharaoh to the afterlife.

17. The Nile River provided a way to move supplies and materials to building sites.

18. Limestone and granite were used to build the pyramids.

19. They face north, south, east, and west.

Hieroglyphs (page 7)

1. Hieroglyphs are the pictures in hieroglyphics, a system of picture writing.

2. A pictogram is a picture that represents an actual object; an ideogram is a picture that represents an idea.

3. sound-signs

4. Communicating with hieroglyphs could be difficult because different people could see the pictures different ways and give them different meanings.

5. The Rosetta stone contained the same passage in two other languages besides hieroglyphics.

Geography, Rulers, and the Afterlife
(pages 8–9)

1. Answers may vary but should mention the desert, waterfalls, and Mediterranean Sea that acted as natural borders.

2. dry sand

3. It was believed that children could play with the toys in the afterlife.

4. Ancient Egyptians believed that their pharaoh was a link to their own afterlife.

5. The process was expensive and time-consuming.

6. Tutankhamen

7. The tomb was hidden for over 3,000 years. Rock chips, left over from the building of a later pharaoh's tomb, had buried it. When Tutankhamen's tomb was discovered in 1922, none of its treasures had been stolen.

8. Answers may vary.

Ancient Greece

Geography and Life (pages 10–11)

1. Mediterranean **2.** Crete **3.** Aegean
4. Italy **5.** Black **6.** Adriatic

Greek Gods and Goddesses (pages 12–13)

1. Zeus ruled over and protected the human race, as well as the Olympian family.

2. Cronus, the father of Zeus, feared that one of his children might dethrone him. He solved his problem by swallowing each one of them as they were born. To save Zeus, his mother, Rhea, wrapped a stone in clothes for Cronus to swallow and hid Zeus on the island of Crete. When Zeus grew up, he forced Cronus to disgorge the other children.

3. Answers may vary.

4. the gift of prophecy

5. Answers may vary.

6. Zeus

7. She sprang from the forehead of Zeus and was already full-grown.

8. Answers may vary.

9. corn and harvest

10. Demeter's daughter, Persephone, was kidnapped but allowed to return to her mother each spring and had to leave her each fall. Demeter was happy in the spring and this made the flowers grow and the harvest abundant. In winter, however, Demeter was sad, and so the vegetation died and there was desolation.

11. dead

12. Answers may vary.

Ancient Olympics (pages 14–15)

1. Answers may vary but might mention that Olympia was green, lush, and set in a grove of trees; or describe the placement of the buildings.

2. a crown of wild olive

3. a footrace

4. 18

5. Answers may vary but might include differences such as fewer rules and the absence of rounds or weight classes.

6. Answers may vary but might include that strength, rhythm, and precision were each important in throwing the discus; and that both the materials and the size of the discus varied.

7. Answers may vary but might include that jumpers used lead or stone weights to increase the length of their jump. These weights were held in front of the jumper during his ascent and then thrust behind his back and dropped during his descent to help further his jump.

8. Answers may vary but might include that races were measured by the length of a stadium. This distance was called a stade and was equal to 192 meters. There were four different races: 1 Stade, 2 Stade, 7–24 Stade, and 2–4 Stade. Even though the last race was relatively short, it was the most difficult because the runners wore armor that weighed 50–60 pounds.

Venn Diagram (page 15)

Sample answers are given.

Ancient Olympics: There were fewer events. Only free men who spoke Greek could compete. An olive crown was worn by the winners. The games were always held at Olympia.

Modern Olympics: There are many more events, including winter events. Any person from any country is eligible to compete. Winning athletes are given medals to wear. A different site is chosen each year the Olympics are held.

Both: Winning athletes are heroes who put their homeland on the map. Winning athletes are recognized. Both are games of athletic skill and sportsmanship.

The Human Body

Body Systems (pages 16–17)

1. 12

2. nervous

3. endocrine

4. The digestive system breaks down food into nutrients and water that can be used by the body.

5. urinary

6. carbon dioxide; oxygen

7. circulatory

8. The immune system battles diseases that could make people sick.

9. lymphatic

10. skeletal

11. muscular

12. integumentary

13. Each body system carries on an important task, which itself depends on other body systems.

Fun Fact

Ancient Egyptians used body parts to measure things.

Fitness (page 18)

1. increased athleticism

2. better posture

3. fat loss

4. improved heart health

5. heightened self-image

6. social benefits

7. intellectual gains

8. enjoyment

9. Answers may vary.

Fitness Do's and Don'ts (page 19)

Do... Start off moderately. Warm up and cool down. Stretch. Consult a trainer. Find a workout partner. Watch what you eat. Have fun.

Don't... Over exercise. Push an injury. Get bored. Lose concentration. Dehydrate yourself.

The Myths of Fitness (page 20)

1. False **2.** True **3.** False **4.** True
5. False **6.** False **7.** False **8.** True
9. False **10.** True **11.** False **12.** False

Heart Rates and Getting Active (pages 20–21)

1. Answers may vary.

2. Answers may vary.

3. between your minimum and maximum heart rate

4. To find a heart rate, first find the pulse, then count heartbeats for six seconds, and finally multiply by 10.

5. Answers may vary.

6. The sport has to be fun for you.

7. Duration, Intensity, Frequency

My Own Food Pyramid (page 22)

Illustrations may vary but should refer to the following servings:

Fats, oils, sweets: use sparingly

Milk, yogurt, cheese: 2–3 servings

Meat, fish, poultry, dry beans, eggs, nuts: 2–3 servings

Vegetables: 3–5 servings

Fruits: 2–4 servings

Bread, cereal, rice, pasta: 6–11 servings

Calorie-Burning Comparison Chart (page 23)

Answers may vary.

Martin Luther King Jr.

The Life of Martin Luther King Jr. (page 24)

1. Martin Luther King Jr. was born.

2. King graduated from Morehouse College in Atlanta, Georgia.

3. King married Coretta Scott.

4. King published his first book, *Stride Toward Freedom*.

5. King met with President John F. Kennedy to urge him to support civil rights.

6. At the March on Washington, King delivered his famous "I Have a Dream" speech.

7. King won the Nobel Peace Prize.

8. King met with President Lyndon B. Johnson about voting rights for African Americans.

9. James Earl Ray assassinated King in Memphis, Tennessee.

10. King's birthday was first celebrated as a national holiday.

Charting the Course of the Civil Rights Movement (page 25)

Answers may vary.

Rosa Parks (page 26)

1. Answers may vary.

2. Detroit

3. 40

4. A boycott of Montgomery buses happened as a result of Rosa Parks's arrest.

5. The boycott lasted 381 days.

6. Answers may vary.

7. 45th

8. Answers may vary.

Think About It... (page 27)

Answers may vary.

The Nine Planets

Facts About the Solar System (page 28)

1. nine; orbits

2. Mercury, Venus, Earth, and Mars

3. The inner planets are closer to the sun, which is in the middle of the solar system, than the outer planets.

4. The asteroid belt separates the inner and the outer planets.

5. Illustrations may vary.

The Planets and Their Characteristics (page 29)

Webs may vary but should mention the following information:

Mercury, Venus, Earth, Mars, and Pluto are known as the rocky planets, as well as the small planets. They are primarily rock and metal, and are very heavy and move slowly. They have very few moons and do not have rings. They are no more than 13,000 kilometers in diameter.

Jupiter, Saturn, Uranus, and Neptune are known as the gas planets, as well as the giant planets. They are primarily hydrogen and helium, and are light, considering their sizes. They move quickly, and have rings and lots of moons. They are at least 48,000 kilometers in diameter.

1. composition; size

2. Answers may vary but should mention that the small and rocky planets are the same, and the giant and gas planets are the same.

The Sun and Inner Planets (page 30–31)

1. A heliocentric system is centered around the sun.

2. photosphere

3. Sunspots are cool regions on the sun, with temperatures of around 3800°K. Their cooler temperature makes them appear darker than the rest of the sun, which is normally 5800°K.

4. In a solar eclipse, light from the sun is blocked off during a short period of time when the moon passes directly between Earth and the sun.

5. The sun is more than a million kilometers in diameter and has a center temperature of 15 million degrees Celsius.

6. *Mariner 10*

7. ice

8. The Caloris Basin was probably created by a crash early in our solar system's history.

9. Answers may vary.

10. Venus, the brightest planet known in ancient times, was also the name of the Roman goddess of love and beauty.

11. Venus's atmosphere contains a large amount of carbon dioxide, which acts like a blanket. Venus gets hotter and stays hot because the heat gets trapped underneath this thick layer of clouds.

12. Answers may vary, but similarities might include their chemical compositions and that they are both about the same size and have few craters. Differences might include that Venus is hotter than Earth and doesn't have a moon.

13. Earth's surface has changed a lot from when it was first formed. Things like earthquakes and erosion still change its surface.

14. Answers may vary but should mention that most of Earth's surface is covered by water, which helps keep Earth's temperature stable. Water can exist in liquid form on Earth only. It's also responsible for erosion and is essential for human life.

15. Seeing Earth from space helps to predict the weather.

16. Red Planet

17. Olympus Mons is a mountain on Mars. It is the largest in the solar system, rising 24 kilometers high and stretching 500 kilometers across.

18. water

The Outer Planets (pages 32–33)

1. Jupiter's different colors are a result of different chemical reactions in its atmosphere.

2. Answers may vary but might include that the Great Red Spot is a high-pressure region, which is a storm of swirling gas that has lasted for hundreds of years. The region is much higher and colder than the surrounding areas.

3. 16

4. Io, Europa, Ganymede, and Callisto

5. Saturn's bands are fainter, and wider near the equator.

6. Saturn's rings are much brighter and are made up of many particles—usually ranging from 1 centimeter to several meters—that each circle Saturn at its own speed.

7. 18

8. Answers may vary.

9. Methane, a gas found in the planet's upper atmosphere, causes the blue color.

10. Because Uranus spins differently, it seems to be tilted sideways.

11. Answers may vary but might include that Neptune has methane in its atmosphere like Uranus. However, Neptune is smaller, but heavier, than Uranus.

12. Scientists think that Neptune's Great Dark Spot has either dissipated or is being hidden by Neptune's atmosphere.

13. Answers may vary but should mention that Pluto is the farthest planet from the sun and has never been visited by a spacecraft.

14. Answers may vary.

Planet Comparisons (page 34)

1. Pluto **2.** 90,520 **3.** Jupiter **4.** 11
5. Mercury and Venus **6.** Pluto
7. Jupiter **8.** Saturn **9.** gravity

The Rain Forest

What's in the Rain Forest? (pages 35–36)

1. Tribal people have taught us about many kinds of medicines and foods.

2. They are used for medicines, both by people in the rain forest and in hospitals throughout the world. Rain forest products are found in one-fourth of the drugs in drugstores.

3. People become ill when they are forced to move into the cities because they can no longer eat their native foods or sleep in their own homes. They are exposed to many new diseases that make them very ill and can cause death.

4. Answers may vary but should refer to the rain forests as the oldest ecosystems on earth and the conditions that are perfect for a large number of different species.

5. You would see millions of insects.

6. Many animals adapt to eating a specific plant or animal.

7. Many animals live in a positive relationship to plants. For example, birds and fish eat the fruit from trees, and, in turn, eating the fruit helps to spread the seeds to different parts of the forest.

8. Camouflage enables the walking stick to blend in with the forest so its enemies have a difficult time finding it and it also helps the boa constrictor by enabling it to sneak up on animals and surprise them.

9. The coral snake, despite its beautiful coloring, has a deadly poison that can quickly kill.

10. Answers may vary but should mention that the hoatzin has a horrible smell.

Think About It... (page 37)

Answers may vary but might mention logging, cattle ranching, trading animals illegally for pets and for their fur, overpopulation, pollution of rivers, and extinction as a natural process.

Rain Forest Layers and Locations (page 38)

1. Answers may vary but might mention that the canopy makes up the ceiling of the rain forest and consists of its treetops. Mainly monkeys and birds live here. The understory is the trees, ferns, and shrubs under the canopy. The forest floor is the bottom of the rain forest and is almost bare, except for the rotting vegetation and the jaguars and gorillas that are found there.

2. Check that students' maps reflect the information found on the Web site.

Think About It... (page 39)

Sample answers given.

Rain forests help to control the world's climate, give off oxygen because of the trees, and absorb carbon dioxide.

Since rainforests have been developing for hundreds of millions of years and contain unique species, it's not possible for them to simply "grow back" to the way they were originally. When the trees are cut down, soil can dry up in the sun and wash away in the rain.

Volcanoes

Earth's Layers (pages 40–41)

1. crust, mantle, outer core, inner core

2. crust

3. basalt and granite

4. nickel and iron

5. 3–5; 5–25

6. 1600

7. plates

8. An earthquake occurs.

9. Basalt is much denser and heavier than granite.

10. It is composed of hot, dense rock and varies in temperature from 1600 to 4000°F.

11. The hottest material in the center of the mantle will rise, cool, and sink repeatedly, causing convection currents.

12. Outer Core: 1,800 miles beneath the crust; about 1,400 miles thick; up to 9000°F.
Inner Core: 4,000 miles beneath the crust; about 800 miles thick; up to 9000°F.

Volcano Facts (page 42)

1. Volcanic activity is the most powerful force in nature.

2. An island called Vulcano lies off the coast of Italy. It was once believed that Vulcan, the Roman god of fire and maker of weapons, used the volcano on that island to make his weapons.

3. active, alive, dormant, resting, sleeping, extinct, dead, lifetime, and restless

4. A volcano is an opening in the crust of Earth through which molten rock called magma and gases can escape to the surface. A volcano is the mountain that is formed from volcanic eruptions.

5. It grew 500 feet in one week in 1943.

6. Active volcanoes are either currently erupting or have erupted in recorded history. Dormant volcanoes are not currently erupting but are likely to do so. Extinct volcanoes have not erupted in recorded history and are not expected to erupt ever again.

7. Answers may vary but should refer to the loss of the summit and the forests, as well as a change in the shape of the lake.

Volcanic Cones and Eruptions (pages 43–45)

1. The magma will rise because it is less dense than the surrounding rock. The gas in the magma will bubble out as it reaches Earth's surface because the pressure surrounding the magma will decrease nearer the surface.

2. Volcanoes are classified according to the type of eruption and their shape.

3. The basic volcanic cone shapes are cinder cones, shield cones, and composite cones.

4. The cone shape becomes steeper as an eruption becomes more violent.

5. Very hot, thin, and runny lava floods the surface of Earth.

6. Shield cones are very low and very broad volcanoes that turn into thick lava plateaus because of the repeated eruptions over the same area.

7. Illustrations may vary but should show characteristics described in the previous answer.

8. A Strombolian eruption, in which very thick lava and bursts of steam and gas are shot into the air, is short lived. A cinder cone is created from a Strombolian eruption.

9. After red-hot magma, cinders, and ash are exploded from the volcano, these materials settle around the main vent and create a steep-sided cone.

10. During a Vulcanian eruption, dark clouds of steam, ash, and gas, resembling a head of cauliflower, appear. Then, after emitting these materials, a thick, pasty lava is ejected. The build up of this matter results in a steep-sided cone, called a composite cone.

11. Mt. St. Helens in Washington; Mt. Rainier in Washington; Mt. Fuji in Japan; Mt. Pinatubo in the Philippines; Mt. Etna in Sicily; Mayon in the Philippines

12. Answers may vary but should mention that a Plinian eruption can spew out gas and ash at more than 70 miles per hour, forming clouds that rise up to heights of 10 miles. They are very deadly eruptions. Examples are Mt. St. Helens in Washington, May 18, 1980, and Mt. Vesuvius in Italy, A.D. 79.

Whales

Whale Facts (pages 46–47)

1. There is insufficient food supply in fresh water for whales.

2. 13

3. Whales tend to swim faster if they are in danger, if they leap out of the water, or if they are at the surface.

4. sperm whale

5. A humpback whale has a hump on its back in front of its dorsal fin, and it arches, or humps, its back when diving.

6. The trachea and esophagus are separate.

7. Whales may have lost their sense of smell when the nostrils moved from the front to the top of the head. For the most part, the blowhole is closed, except when the whale breathes at the surface.

8. Whales would suffocate if they went into a deep sleep because they need to be conscious in order to breathe.

9. On long dives, bottlenose and sperm whales can stay underwater for nearly two hours. Other whales, such as the blue and fin whales, usually surface within 40 minutes.

10. 30 years

11. 50 years

12. 65–70 years

13. They carry too much blubber for tropical waters.

All About Whales (pages 49–50)

Venn Diagram

Sample facts are given.

Gray Whales

Size: Females reach lengths of 45 feet and weigh up to 70,000 pounds. Males tend to be smaller.

Eating Habits: They eat food found at the bottom of the ocean.

Location: They spend summers in the Bering, Chukchi, and Beaufort seas and migrate to warmer waters during the winter.

Other: They are often called "friendly whales" because they approach small boats.

Killer Whales

Size: Females can reach lengths of 24 feet and weigh between 3,000 to 8,000 pounds. Males can reach lengths of 27 feet and weigh up to 12,000 pounds.

Eating Habits: They eat fish, squid, seals, sea lions, penguins, and other whales.

Location: They are found in every ocean.

Other: They have sharp teeth, which produce growth layers. A whale's age can be determined by counting these layers.

Blue Whales

Size: As the largest whale species, they can reach lengths of 69 to 78 feet. They can weigh 142,000 pounds, on average.

Eating Habits: As filter feeders, they eat krill, which is a small shrimp-like animal.

Location: They are found in every ocean.

Other: Blue whales can gain as much as 200 pounds a day during their first eight months.

The White House

Washington, D.C. (page 51)

1. 1600 Pennsylvania Avenue

2. the Lincoln Memorial, the Jefferson Memorial, and the Washington Monument

3. Potomac River

4. south; west; east; north

5. George Washington

6. It was centrally located between the northern and southern states.

7. There were marshy areas, pigs roaming the streets, and many mosquitoes.

White House Facts (pages 52–53)

1. the Civil War

2. William Henry Harrison

3. His term lasted 32 days.

4. 1792

5. John Adams

6. British soldiers set fire to the White House.

7. She saved important papers and a portrait of George Washington.

8. 6,000

9. 6; 132; 32; 412

10. Theodore Roosevelt named the White House in 1901.

11. White House Christmas tree

12. green silk

13. red satin

14. East Room

15. The president carries out business relating to the country.

The People and Pets (pages 53–54)

1. It was a pony.

2. Tad Lincoln once made all of the White House bells ring at the same time.

3. Buddy is a chocolate lab that arrived in 1997.

4. Socks, the cat belonging to the Clintons, moved into the White House in 1993.

5. Russell Harrison had a goat.

6. Answers may vary.

7. Answers may vary.

The Presidents (page 55)

Answers may vary.

Wolves

Wolf Facts (pages 56–58)

1. Five subspecies of gray wolf are currently found in North America.

2. Answers may vary but might mention skull dimensions, overall size, fur color, and the length of appendages.

3. A pack usually includes the adult parents and their offspring of maybe the last two or three years.

4. Generally six to eight wolves are in a pack, but may reach as many as 30 in northwest Alaska and Canada.

5. The birth of pups, dispersal, and mortality rates affect pack size.

6. Wolves are normally born in spring.

7. An average litter contains six pups.

8. Northwestern Minnesota: Adult males weigh between 70 and 110 pounds. Adult females weigh between 50 and 85 pounds. Northwestern United States, Canada, and Alaska: Adult males weigh between 85 and 115 pounds. Adult females generally weigh 10 to 15 pounds less than the males.

9. Answers may vary but might include the existence of larger food supplies or wolves being on the protected list.

10. Answers may vary but might include white-tailed deer, mule deer, moose, elk, caribou, bison, Dall sheep, musk oxen, or mountain goats.

11. Answers may vary but might include beaver, snowshoe hare, small mammals, and birds.

12. Answers may vary.

13. A wolf needs five pounds of food per day to reproduce successfully.

14. A wolf needs a minimum of 17.5 pounds of food in a week in order to survive, or 2.5 pounds per day.

15. 15–18

16. A wolf can reach a speed of 25–35 miles per hour while chasing prey.

17. Answers may vary but might mention that since wolves need 2.5 pounds of food each day, they may travel 10–30 miles in a day in order to find this amount of food.

18. They live longer in captivity. This may be because there is a guaranteed food supply.

How Wolves Communicate (pages 58–59)

1. Wolves use body language.

2. A pack is made up of leaders and followers.

3. Alpha wolves are usually the oldest, largest, strongest, and most intelligent wolves in the pack. They are the leaders and act as the mother and father of the pack.

4. They carry their tails high and stand tall.

5. Illustrations may vary.

6. When wolves mark their territories with urine and scats, it is referred to as scent-marking. Scents also tell wolves when food or enemies are near and whether land is occupied by another pack.

7. Wolves howl to find other pack members, to let wolves from outside of the pack know their territory boundaries, or to get the pack excited and ready to hunt.

8. sound, special scents, and body language

9. Answers may vary but might include facial expressions, hand gestures, or body movements.

Crossword Puzzle (page 60)

Across 3. Abyssinian **4.** body **6.** deer
8. scent-marking **9.** pups **11.** alpha
13. five **14.** litter **15.** angry

Down 1. subordinate **2.** beavers **4.** bark
5. starvation **6.** down **7.** dominance
10. prey **12.** Alaska **13.** fear